Shark
EXPEDITION
A SHARK PHOTOGRAPHER'S CLOSE ENCOUNTERS

by Mary M. Cerullo

Photographs by Jeffrey L. Rotman

Consultant: James Sulikowski, PhD
Marine Science Department, University of New England

CAPSTONE YOUNG READERS
a capstone imprint

Compass Point Books are published by Capstone,
1710 Roe Crest Drive, North Mankato, Minnesota 56003
www.capstonepub.com

Library of Congress Cataloging-in-Publication Data
Cerullo, Mary M., author.
Shark expedition: a shark photographer's close encounters / by Mary M. Cerullo.
pages cm.—(Capstone young readers)
Summary: "Provides information about many species of sharks and shares a shark diver's
experiences searching for and photographing them"—Provided by publisher.
Audience: Ages 11 to 15.
Audience: Grades 5 to 9.
Includes bibliographical references and index.
ISBN 978-1-62370-156-7 (paperback)
1. Rotman, Jeffrey L.—Juvenile literature. 2. Sharks—Juvenile literature. 3. Wildlife photography—
Juvenile literature. 4. Underwater photography—Juvenile literature. 5. Wildlife photographers—
Juvenile literature. I. Title.
QL638.9.C3685 2015
597.3—dc23   2014024953

Editorial Credits
Kristen Mohn, editor; Veronica Scott, designer; Svetlana Zhurkin, media researcher;
Tori Abraham, production specialist

Photo Credits
All photographs by Jeffrey L. Rotman with the exception of:
Adam Rotman, 116; Asher Gal, 72 (inset), 129; Avi Klapfer, 109; Dreamstime: Flavijus, 22; Isabelle
Delafosse, 3, 142 (bottom); Rodney Fox, 49 (top); Shutterstock: Alfonso de Tomas, 45, amorfati.art,
110, Andreas Meyer, 60, KUCO, 43, Leonardo Gonzalez, 128, Machkazu, 61, Olinchuk, 77 (bottom),
Pjard, 8, ronfromyork, 89, Sergey Dubrov, 113 (bottom), Sergey Uryadnikov, 62 (inset), Sergiy
Zavgorodny, 29, tororo reaction, 86–87, Volina, 94 (right)
Design Elements by Shutterstock

Printed in China.
092014 008474RRDS15

TABLE OF CONTENTS

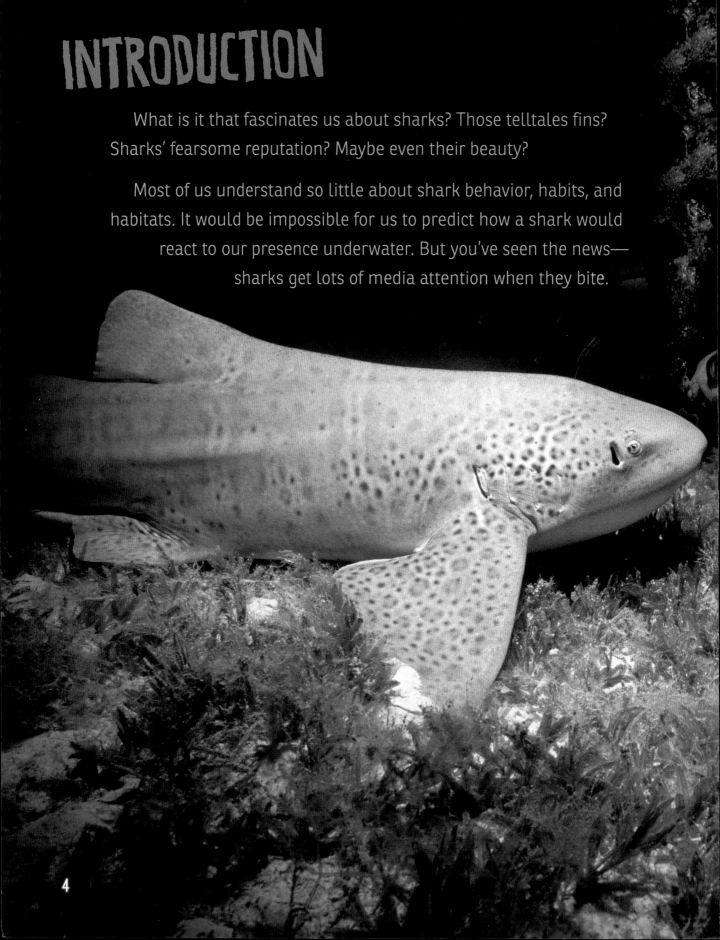

INTRODUCTION

What is it that fascinates us about sharks? Those telltales fins? Sharks' fearsome reputation? Maybe even their beauty?

Most of us understand so little about shark behavior, habits, and habitats. It would be impossible for us to predict how a shark would react to our presence underwater. But you've seen the news— sharks get lots of media attention when they bite.

(Don't worry—you've only got about a one in 11.5 million chance of being attacked by a shark.) Sure, they can be dangerous, but there's so much more to a shark than its teeth.

Jeffrey L. Rotman has spent a lifetime getting to know these creatures. He has been pursuing them for more than 40 years—with his camera. Jeff specializes in taking close-up photos of marine life, especially sharks. He has come to understand his "prey" by spending time with scientists, fishermen, and conservationists. He has also spent countless hours underwater watching both well-known and rarely seen sharks in nearly every ocean of the world.

You don't need scuba gear or a shark cage to get up close with sharks. Through Jeff's lens you can look as much as you dare.

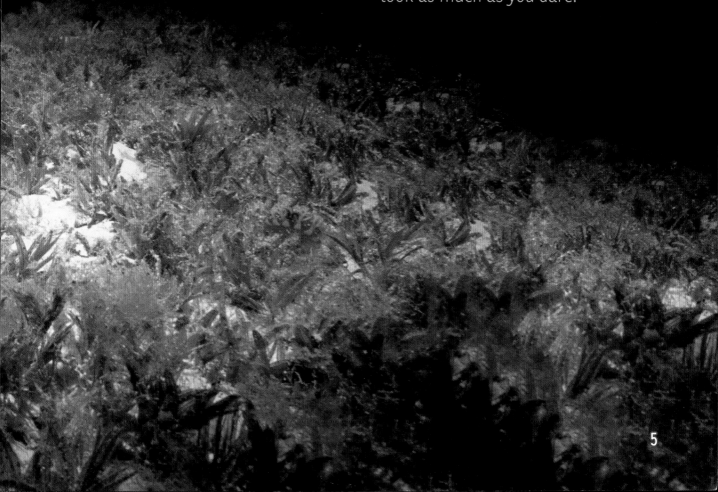

LIVING SCULPTURES

Jeffrey Rotman's career as an underwater photographer drives him to get as close as he can to every sea creature he meets. That brings him face-to-face with many fish—including sharks—and he loves it.

Why sharks, people may ask? "Sharks get such bad press," Jeff replies. "Everyone concentrates on the few big ones that occasionally mistake a human for a seal. You have to look at sharks differently. I see them as living sculptures, especially the bottom sharks and their relatives, the skates and rays. They have an incredible variety of faces, jaws, and shapes. These ocean floor fishes haven't gotten the attention they deserve."

A diver is face-to-face with a bigeye hound shark.

TOP 10 REASONS JEFF LOVES TO DIVE:

1. Meeting cool fish—especially sharks

2. Meeting cool scientists and watching how they work

3. Traveling the world

4. Becoming part of another world

5. Finding something the whole family can do together (if you're Jeff's family!)

6. Making friends for life with dive companions

7. Using really cool (though expensive) equipment

8. Learning valuable lessons—such as don't step on a panther torpedo ray

9. Learning how to become like a fish

10. Using photography and diving skills to help protect sharks, rays, and other ocean life

WHERE IT ALL BEGAN

Even though Jeff Rotman has swum in nearly every ocean in the world, the coast of Cape Ann, Massachusetts, is still one of his favorite underwater habitats. It's where he made his first ocean dive.

It was no easy task. Jeff and his dive companion had to scramble over rocks and through crashing waves just to get to the water. They wore wetsuits, weight belts, face masks, fins, and three-fingered gloves called lobster claws to keep their hands warm in the chilly water.

One thing he was not wearing was a scuba tank. Jeff learned to free dive first—a more athletic sport, he feels, than diving with an air supply. He plunged to about 25 feet (7.6 meters) and stayed down for a minute before returning to the surface for air.

As you dive deeper into the water, the temperature also drops—to about 40 degrees Fahrenheit (4.5 degrees Celsius). "When you dive beneath the surface here, the water is green, dark, and cold. There is almost zero visibility," Jeff says. "Once you learn to dive in those conditions, you can dive anywhere." And Jeff has.

Cape Ann, Massachusetts

FREE DIVING

Over time, as Jeff got better at free diving, he was able to stay down for two minutes or even longer. His advice: First, you must be very comfortable in the water. (Jeff even uses yoga breathing exercises to help him relax.) Then you train to hold your breath through lots of practice. He recommends practicing in a swimming pool and swimming laps underwater. Jeff also suggests other sports, such as running, to make you physically fit, because free diving is an extremely demanding activity.

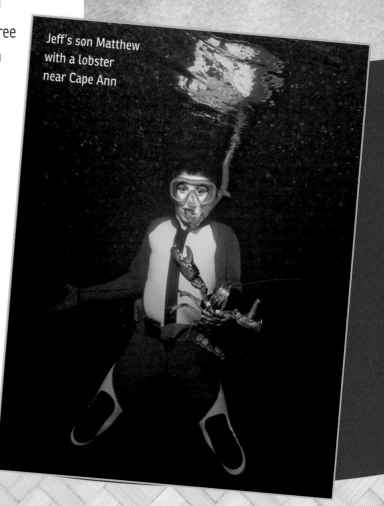

Jeff's son Matthew with a lobster near Cape Ann

yellowtail flounder

FACT:

Because the water is so cold and murky, fewer people dive in New England than in clear tropical seas. But they miss meeting some fascinating creatures lurking in these waters, such as flounder, lobsters, goosefish, and striped bass.

Eventually Jeff started using a scuba tank so he could go deeper—as far as 100 feet (30 m) down. There he poked among the kelp beds, discovering creatures such as sea ravens, wolf eels, sea stars, horseshoe crabs, and giant sea anemones. He learned from field guides, fishermen, and other divers that there were many sharks in these waters, especially small dogfish sharks that often travel in huge schools. Yet they never allowed Jeff to spot them.

The sand tiger shark gets its name from trolling the sand near the ocean floor, hunting for prey.

The only sharks Jeff encountered were the ones swimming in the Giant Ocean Tank at the New England Aquarium in Boston. There he joined staff divers to feed fearsome-looking sand tiger sharks by hand. Long, sharp teeth that stuck out beyond their jaws made them aquarium favorites. But looks can be deceiving. Jeff discovered that sand tiger sharks are quite easygoing in captivity.

After swimming with the sand tigers, Jeff was more determined than ever to meet a shark in the wild.

SAND TIGER SHARK STATS

AVERAGE LENGTH
6.5 to 9 feet (2 to 2.7 m)

APPROXIMATE WEIGHT
200 to 300 pounds (91 to 136 kilograms)

RANGE
worldwide, near the ocean floor

DIET
mostly bony fish, skates, and other sharks

DIVING THE RED SEA
HAMMERHEADS AND STINGRAYS

Jeff once asked the famous underwater explorer Jacques Cousteau to name his favorite place to dive. "My happiest hours have been spent beneath the waters of the Red Sea," Cousteau replied. It became one of Jeff's favorite places too. In fact, it was there that Jeff met his first shark outside of an aquarium.

It was a scalloped hammerhead—actually, three of them together. They were curious and came within 20 feet (6 m) to check Jeff out. It was a frightening experience, because at the time, all hammerheads had the reputation of being man-eaters. (We now know that is false—only the great hammerhead is dangerous.) So when Jeff saw not just one, but three huge hammerheads coming toward him, his heart started to race. And because things are magnified underwater, they looked even bigger than they were!

The slight curves along the front of the scalloped hammerhead's face help distinguish it from the great hammerhead.

SCALLOPED HAMMERHEAD STATS

AVERAGE LENGTH
10 to 12 feet (3 to 3.7 m)

MAXIMUM LENGTH
14 feet (4.3 m)

MAXIMUM WEIGHT
336 pounds (152 kg)

RANGE
tropical Atlantic and Pacific oceans
and tropical seas

LIFE SPAN
more than 30 years

DIET
mostly fish, especially small stingrays,
sardines, mackerel, and herring

Jeff returns to the Red Sea every year to see the sharks and to dive with two of his children, Adam and Dana, who love the Red Sea as much as he does. Jeff taught all his children to free dive when they were each about 5 years old. Eventually they began to use scuba gear as well.

The Rotman kids learned at an early age which sea creatures they could approach and which were dangerous. They knew that a stingray's venomous spine could inject venom if another animal tried to attack it. They also knew that the stingray only uses its spine to defend itself. As long as the stingray isn't bothered, it should have no need to use its stinger.

When Jeff's son Adam was 11, he came upon a blue-spotted stingray as he was free diving in about 20 feet (6 m) of water. Being a good photographer's son, Adam dove again and again, getting to within inches of the dangerous ray, to make sure his dad got the photo he wanted. The blue-spotted ray did not try to bury itself in the sand as many stingrays do. In fact, it stood its ground as Adam came closer and closer until finally, after several minutes, it got tired of posing and fluttered away.

Jeff's son Adam poses with a blue-spotted stingray

BLUE-SPOTTED STINGRAY STATS

MAXIMUM DISC WIDTH
14 inches (36 centimeters)

AVERAGE WEIGHT
11 pounds (5 kg)

RANGE
tropical Indian and western Pacific oceans, in
coral reefs or nearby sandy shallows; rarely
found deeper than 100 feet (30 m)

DIET
snails, clams, crabs, worms, and shrimp

FACT:

Its bright blue colors have made the blue-spotted
stingray too popular for its own good. People want
to keep these beautiful creatures as aquarium
pets, but they don't live long in captivity. Now
blue-spotted rays are becoming rare.

Rays and skates are members of a special branch of the shark family. Scientists estimate that there are about 500 kinds of rays. They range from the short-nose electric ray, which is about the size and shape of a pancake, to the magnificent manta ray, which can grow to be more than 20 feet (6 m) across.

In shallow water stingrays can present a problem to beachgoers. Tourists walking along the shores of the Red Sea are warned to shuffle their feet to scare up hidden rays.

manta ray, the largest of rays

A panther torpedo ray uses camouflage to hide in the sand, ready to surprise prey.

Jeff forgot that lesson one time and stepped on a panther torpedo ray. He got a shock from the electric ray that nearly knocked him off his feet. Some bottom sharks and rays can generate a strong electrical discharge to stun prey or predators. A shock can deliver up to 200 volts—nearly twice the voltage of a typical household electrical outlet. "And once you get such a shock—whether you're human or fish—you remember it!" Jeff says.

MADE FOR LIFE AT THE BOTTOM

Imagine squashing a shark so flat that it would fit against the ocean bottom. In a way, that is what nature has done with the ray and its relatives, which evolved from sharks.

A skeleton of flexible cartilage supports a ray's winglike side fins. The fins, which are much wider than a shark's, can press flat against the ocean bottom.

A ray's eyes sit on top of its head.

If a ray took water in through its mouth, as most fish do, it would choke on sand. Instead water goes through openings on the top of its head, called spiracles. Even when a ray buries itself up to its eyeballs, its spiracles poke above the sand.

A ray's mouth is on its bottom side. Rows of flat, grinding teeth help a ray crunch bottom-dwelling crabs, spiny lobsters, clams, and snails.

A ray's carefully concealed bottom side has lost all coloration, and its topside blends in perfectly with the ocean floor to hide it from predators above.

LOOKING DEEPER
PYGMY AND HOUND SHARKS

To learn more about deepwater sharks and other creatures, Jeff joined an expedition of ocean scientists from Eilat, Israel, who were studying the marine life in the depths of the Red Sea. Their equipment could go much deeper than a human diver ever could.

The researchers lowered baited fishing lines and barbless hooks to the ocean floor, more than a half-mile below the surface. After many hours they raised the lines very slowly, so that deep-sea creatures used to living under extreme pressure could adjust to the lesser pressure at the surface. Jeff was one of the first people to meet—and photograph—the rare Moses smoothhound shark and the bigeye hound shark. The name bigeye fits—the deepwater sharks have huge eyes to pick up any faint light that glimmers from other deep-sea animals. Since they mostly feed on bottom creatures, having their mouth underneath allows them to easily graze for food on the ocean floor.

THE PRESSURE IS ON

The deeper you dive into the ocean, the greater the pressure you feel from the weight of the water above you. At a depth of 3,000 feet (914 m), the water pressure is enough to squeeze a piece of wood to half its size. Even the most experienced scuba divers can only dive to about 300 feet (91 m) before the water pressure becomes too much.

Moses smoothhound shark

bigeye hound shark

The bigeye hound shark is part of the hound shark family. There are about 30 species of hound sharks.

Jeff also went to sea with scientists from the University of Haifa in Israel to explore the bottom of the Mediterranean Sea on the other side of the Suez Canal from the Red Sea. Their nets pulled up a strange sea creature from a depth of 3,000 feet (914 m). Rows of tiny light organs on its belly emitted a faint glow, like a firefly. Perhaps these lights were meant to attract the attention of unsuspecting prey in the deep ocean. The fish had huge eyes, likely used to see prey such as squid and other fish that also produce their own living light. Imagine how bright the sun must have seemed to a "lightning bug" from the bottom of the sea.

The exotic specimen was a spined pygmy shark, about 8 inches (20 cm) long. Although it is one of the smallest sharks in the world, it ranks as the top predator in the ocean food chain of the deep Mediterranean.

SPINED PYGMY SHARK STATS

AVERAGE LENGTH
6 to 8 inches (15 to 20 cm)

MAXIMUM LENGTH
12 inches (31 cm)

RANGE
temperate and tropical oceans
and seas worldwide

DIET
deepwater squid, shrimp, and small fish

The spined pygmy is also known as the bigeye dwarf shark.

WORKING THE NIGHT SHIFT
NURSE SHARKS

When Jeff Rotman goes to the islands, he doesn't hang out on the beach like the sunbathers do. He heads straight for more interesting stretches of sand beneath the ocean. There he meets the most engaging creatures. On a trip to the Bahamas, Jeff made friends with a "local"—a nurse shark.

The nurse shark didn't seem to mind Jeff's company, possibly because nurse sharks often gather in groups. Sometimes they even sit on top of one another, creating big piles of nurse sharks. Or perhaps the nurse shark was more interested in napping. While many sharks have to keep moving to push enough water over their gills to breathe, a nurse shark can pump water over its gills as it lays motionless on the ocean floor.

Like many bottom sharks and rays, the nurse shark is nocturnal. During the day it rests on the ocean floor, only springing into action if an unsuspecting crab or snail wanders too close to resist. At night a nurse shark rouses itself to actively hunt for food.

A nurse shark has barbels, which are two pieces of skin that hang from its upper jaw like a droopy moustache. These barbels can feel and taste, to help the shark find food in the sand as it cruises along the ocean floor.

A nurse shark can also vacuum up its prey. It cups its mouth over the opening of a small cave or crevice and sucks out a tasty crab or octopus. It's even been known to yank snails right out of their shells.

Nurse sharks tend to ignore humans, but a diver who accidentally steps on one may get a bite from the shark's tiny but strong teeth.

NURSE SHARK STATS

AVERAGE LENGTH
7 to 9 feet (2 to 2.7 m)

MAXIMUM LENGTH
10 feet (3 m)

AVERAGE WEIGHT
200 to 330 pounds (91 to 150 kg)

RANGE
Atlantic coast from Carolinas to Florida Keys,
Gulf of Mexico, and Caribbean

DIET
crabs, shrimp, squid, and small fish

STINGRAY CITY

One of Jeff's oldest friends is Neal Watson. Neal runs dive resorts throughout the Caribbean. Neal was the first scuba diver to reach a depth of 437 feet (133 m), which put him into the *Guinness Book of World Records*.

Neal and his two sons, Neal Jr., 12, and John, 13, planned a trip to the Cayman Islands to swim with stingrays. Neal invited Jeff to come along and to bring his camera. Jeff arrived at the airport with eight large suitcases filled with photographic equipment, dive gear, and two bathing suits.

Together they flew to a string of islands in the western Caribbean Sea. Near the largest island, Grand Cayman, is a lagoon where local fishermen come to clean their catch after a day of fishing. They dump the unwanted fish parts overboard into the shallow bay. Southern stingrays discovered this free food and started showing up regularly. Soon the bay became known as Stingray City.

southern stingray

A SHARK PHOTOGRAPHER'S PACKING LIST

Dive Gear:

several wet suits of varying thicknesses, two masks, a snorkel, a buoyancy compensator vest, weight belt with weights, and fins

Camera Gear:

dive lights, eight cameras, three camera housings to protect cameras from the water, four strobes for underwater flash to restore the natural color, and various camera lenses

Safety Gear:

a compass, a depth gauge, a dive knife, a safety orange strobe for night dives, and a safety sausage tube to wave at the surface in case of separation from the dive boat

Onboard Equipment:

a laptop to download photos from the camera, back-up equipment for everything, including extra batteries for cameras and strobes, and a few good books to read between dives

Every morning dozens of stingrays visit the lagoon to take handouts of squid from tourist divers. The rays swim from dive boat to dive boat, like trick-or-treaters going door-to-door, begging for candy. The stingrays eagerly crowd around each diver, waiting for their treat. Although tourists are warned to watch out for the venomous spines of the stingrays, the animals only use them for defense, never to attack. While most rays move on after getting a piece of squid, some stingrays play tricks to get even more. One stingray knocked off a diver's mask, making her drop her bag of bait in surprise. As if on cue, another ray rushed in to gobble up the goodies!

To make sure they would get good photographs of the stingrays with the boys, Jeff and Neal stuffed handfuls of squid inside the pockets of the boys' dive vests. But the delicious smell sent the stingrays into a feeding frenzy once the boys hit the water. The overexcited rays dive-bombed them to try to get at the food. The boys quickly retreated to the boat and dug the squid out of their vests. They decided to take a different approach.

Back underwater, they held out pieces of squid in their hands. Now the stingrays approached more politely. The boys spent the next several hours happily petting and playing with the stingrays, lifting them from underneath to avoid the venomous spines.

The Watsons dive with stingrays.

SOUTHERN STINGRAY STATS

AVERAGE WIDTH
females 4 feet (1.2 m),
males 2 to 3 feet (61 to 91 cm)

MAXIMUM WIDTH
5 feet (1.5 m)

RANGE
Atlantic Ocean, from New Jersey
to Brazil, throughout Caribbean

DIET
mollusks, worms, shrimp,
crabs, and small fish

JEFF'S SHARK CLOSE-UPS FROM AROUND THE (BOTTOM OF THE) WORLD

EASTERN FIDDLER RAY:

sometimes called banjo sharks, fiddlers are members of the shovelnose group of rays

ZEBRA SHARK:

once it reaches adulthood, small dots replace its stripes

SPOTTED EAGLE RAY:

able to leap completely out of the water to escape a predator

WOBBEGONG SHARK:

may look lazy and harmless, but if you don't treat it with respect, it will grab onto you with its powerful jaws and not let go

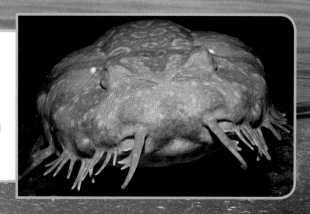

PORT JACKSON SHARK:

sports a spine on its dorsal fin, which it stabs into any predator that tries to swallow it

EPAULETTE SHARK:

like a badge on a military uniform, the shark has a big black oval on its shoulder that would-be predators may mistake for a giant eye

CALIFORNIA HORN SHARK:

has a powerful sense of smell, thanks to many folds of skin inside its nostrils

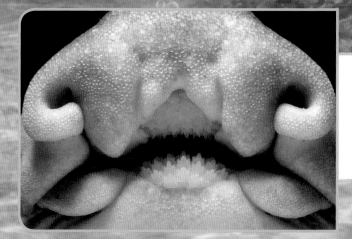

A NEW GENERATION OF DIVERS

Jeff often returns to his favorite place off Cape Ann, Massachusetts, to share its mysteries with his younger sons Matthew and Thomas. Like their dad, the boys are skilled divers. And like their dad, they feel at home in the rough, chilly waters of the North Atlantic Ocean. They are even better than their father at spying animals camouflaged against sand and seaweed, such as lobsters, moon snails, and bottom fish.

On one dive the spiracles of a little skate buried in the coarse sandy bottom caught the boys' eagle-eyed attention. They watched it for a while, but it wasn't until Thomas reached down to grab the skate that it finally tried to escape. Thomas was too quick, though, and caught it by its tail. He knew that skates don't have a venomous spine at the base of their tail like most stingrays.

Flapping its wings as hard as it could, the little skate swiveled its eyes around to see what creature had seized it. Thomas gently turned the skate over, and both boys took turns running their gloved fingers over the rows of small teeth that munch on crabs, sea urchins, and squid.

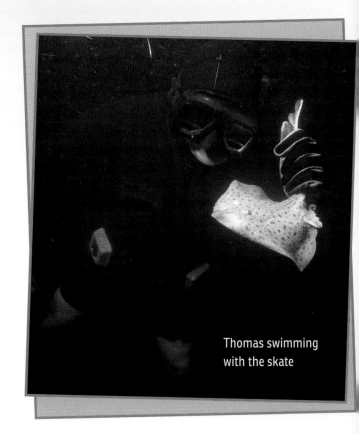

Thomas swimming with the skate

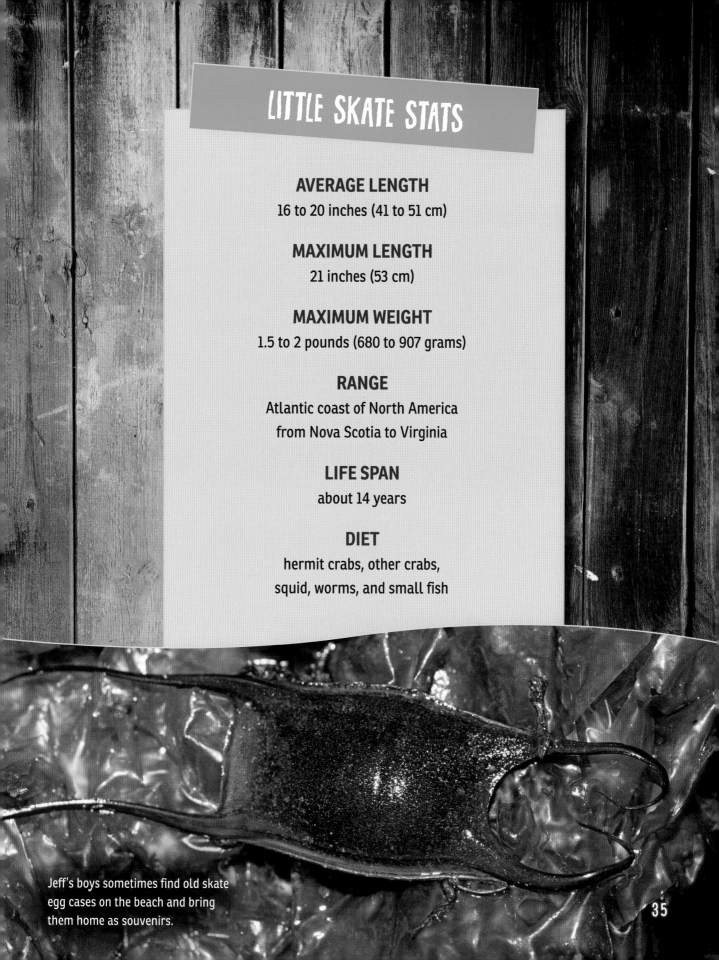

LITTLE SKATE STATS

AVERAGE LENGTH
16 to 20 inches (41 to 51 cm)

MAXIMUM LENGTH
21 inches (53 cm)

MAXIMUM WEIGHT
1.5 to 2 pounds (680 to 907 grams)

RANGE
Atlantic coast of North America
from Nova Scotia to Virginia

LIFE SPAN
about 14 years

DIET
hermit crabs, other crabs,
squid, worms, and small fish

Jeff's boys sometimes find old skate egg cases on the beach and bring them home as souvenirs.

Because many rays and bottom sharks live near coastlines where humans also like to visit, there are bound to be accidental encounters between the species. But many aquariums actually encourage humans and rays to interact by providing opportunities to pet these flattened sharks.

At the New England Aquarium in Boston, Massachusetts, visitors can gently stroke cownose rays, Atlantic rays, and epaulette sharks as they glide around a shallow pool that recreates a coastal mangrove. The exhibit explains how stingrays are important parts of the ocean food web, feeding on other bottom dwellers such as clams, crabs, and small fish. Rays are favorite meals for many kinds of sharks.

yellow stingray

southern stingray

But aquarium exhibit designers most want people to appreciate the adaptations that make these sharks so unique: their shapes, skin patterns, and behavior. Once a stingray comes to the surface and allows you to pet it, you will never feel afraid of one again.

SHARING A PASSION FOR SHARKS

"The ocean is a bridge between my children and me," Jeff says. "Diving is a shared experience that takes us away from our everyday world. It's also a connection with my dive friends and the people I meet who are working to protect sharks and other sea creatures."

Jeff believes in sharing his passion with everyone he can. His photography is another bridge—one between sea animals and humans, providing us a glimpse of the wonders found underwater. The better we understand and appreciate what's below, the better we can help ensure that deep-sea creatures will be swimming far into the future.

A LIFE UNDERWATER

When people learn that Jeff Rotman is an underwater photographer, they always ask, "How do you keep the sharks away?" Jeff jokes, "The best way to scare a shark away is to jump into the water with a camera!"

A better question for Jeff might be, how do you get the sharks to come to you? He knows from experience that most sharks are timid. Jeff has traveled more than 800,000 miles (1.3 million kilometers) to find and photograph more than 100 different kinds of sharks and rays.

In 40 years of diving, Jeff has found his own ways of coaxing sharks to come to him:

1. Learn their habits—their migration patterns, where they hunt, and how deep they live.

2. Wait—sometimes for a very … long … time.

3. Offer treats. (Their favorite foods are fish heads and squashed sardines.)

"Being a good diver is the number one requirement for being a shark photographer. Even so, don't get so comfortable underwater that you forget where you are," Jeff warns. "Never underestimate the shark or overestimate your diving ability."

A diver feeds sharks to get them to pose for photos.

MR. BIG

If you asked Jeff to name his favorite shark, he wouldn't hesitate: a great white. "There is no other shark that can match a great white shark in size, personality, and power," he said. "It's the only shark I've ever seen that sticks its head out of the water and looks right at you." Scientists believe great whites likely developed this behavior to spy on sea lions sunning themselves on the rocks. Jeff says that when one stares at you with those huge black eyes, "you know that it is checking you out."

Jeff refers to the great white as Mr. Big. "Where other sharks are sleek, this one is brawny, like a football player." Its size and strength help a great white shark bring down a hefty adversary, such as a sea lion or an elephant seal. Imagine being chased down by a predator as big as the family car.

GREAT WHITE SHARK STATS

AVERAGE LENGTH
15 feet (4.6 meters)

MAXIMUM LENGTH
21 feet (6.4 m)

MAXIMUM WEIGHT
5,000 pounds (2,268 kilograms)

RANGE
most often found in cool coastal waters,
but they roam worldwide

LIFE SPAN
about 30 years

DIET
fish, squid, dolphins, sea turtles, fur seals,
elephant seals, sea lions, whale calves,
and dead whales

FOLLOW THE FOOD

To find a shark, you must go where the food is. Great white sharks prefer blubbery sea lions, seals, and dead or dying whales. Eating plump prey can sustain a great white for weeks or even a month. Between meals it can live off the fat stored in its liver.

The fur and blubber of these prey marine mammals keep them warm in cold seas. And eating the blubber provides the energy that great whites need to digest their food quickly. It also makes their muscles react fast enough to catch quick swimmers such as seals and dolphins.

GUADALUPE ISLAND

Great white sharks know the best hunting spots are where seals, sea lions, and other marine mammals have their young.

A Galápagos sea lion does a backflip for the camera.

Scientists have learned that great whites can travel far to find their favorite foods. At various times of the year, you can find them in different parts of the world:

February to April
Dangerous Reef, Australia, to eat sea lions

May to September
Dyer Island and Seal Island, South Africa, to eat Cape fur seals

August to December
Guadalupe Island, Mexico, to eat northern elephant seals, California sea lions, and Guadalupe fur seals

Sharks don't have blubber. So how do great whites cope with the chilly water? Unlike cold-blooded fish, which take on the temperature of the surrounding water, great white sharks can raise and maintain their body temperature so that it's warmer than the water around them.

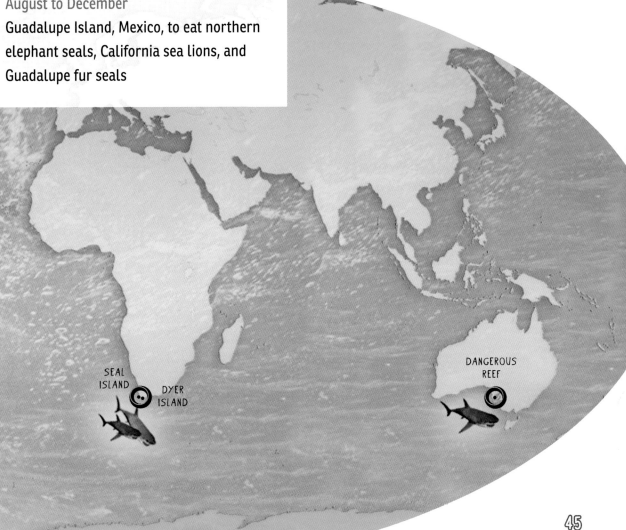

SEAL ISLAND
DYER ISLAND
DANGEROUS REEF

Divers have to stay warm too. Like most divers, Jeff wears a wetsuit that covers him from head to toe. A little bit of seawater seeps inside the suit when he enters the water. His body warms the water, because humans are warm-blooded, maintaining a constant body temperature of 98.6°F (37°C). But after a while, the surrounding water, even in tropical seas, draws the warmth away. Then Jeff has to take a break to get warmed up on the deck of the boat.

Fish don't have eyelids, but many sharks have special coverings that slide over their eyes when they attack. The coverings protect them from the sharp claws of a fur seal or the tusks of an elephant seal.

tiger shark eye

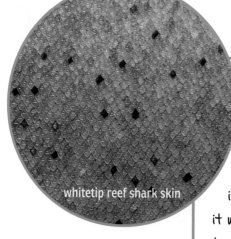
whitetip reef shark skin

FACT:

A shark doesn't feel like other fish. Instead of scales, its body is covered with denticles that give the skin a rough, sandpapery feel. A shark's skin is made from the same material as its teeth. All the denticles point backward, so if you were to run your hand along a shark from snout to tail, it would feel smooth. If you rubbed it the other way—ouch! A tough hide is one way that a shark protects itself in the ocean.

MAKE LIKE A FISH

Jeff knows he must look odd to other underwater creatures. No fish requires so much equipment or has air bubbles gurgling up from a scuba tank. In order to make sharks comfortable with him—and to make himself comfortable in their world—Jeff works hard to become more like a fish.

Flippers act like fins for swimming, turning, or staying upright in the water.

Instead of gills, Jeff has an air tank to breathe underwater.

Goggles imitate a shark's glassy eyeballs.

A wetsuit not only keeps Jeff warm—it helps to protect him if he scrapes against rocks, corals, or the rough skin of a shark.

Jeff's knife acts like a shark's teeth and can be used to free him from a fishing net if needed.

JEFF'S FIRST ENCOUNTER
DANGEROUS REEF, AUSTRALIA

For many years Jeff dreamed of photographing a great white shark. Although great white sharks are found worldwide, they are not common anywhere.

Jeff knew if anyone could help him find a great white shark, it would be Australian conservationist Rodney Fox.

Few people understand great whites better than this man, who survived a great white shark attack. Despite the attack, he has become one of the champions working to protect these animals. And they need protection—scientists estimate there are only about 200 great whites left along Australia's southern coast.

RODNEY'S GREAT WHITE RUN-IN

Rodney Fox is perhaps the most famous shark attack victim ever. As a young man, he was attacked by a great white during a spearfishing contest. He barely survived. Doctors pieced him back together like a jigsaw puzzle, using 462 stitches and 6 pints (2.8 liters) of blood.

After the attack Rodney hated great white sharks and wanted to kill them all. In time, though, he realized that they are important predators in the ocean. Sharks target prey that is easy to catch, such as sick, weak, or dying animals. Rodney calls great whites "the great feeding and cleaning machines of the deep."

Today Rodney takes scientists and photographers to meet great white sharks so that they can understand them better and educate others. Rodney also tracks the numbers of great whites in southern Australia. He tags them so they can be identified when they are seen in other places and in other years. He recognizes many sharks by sight, identifying them by their color patterns or notches in their fins.

Despite almost being killed by a great white shark, Rodney Fox is one of the biggest protectors of the species.

Rodney Fox today holding pictures of himself after the attack

February, March, and April are summer months in Australia. That is when great white sharks come to visit, so that was the perfect time for Jeff to visit too. Jeff journeyed to a place in southern Australia called Dangerous Reef, to join an expedition led by Rodney and Rodney's son Andrew. Also on this trip was famous filmmaker Stan Waterman, who was shooting a movie on great white sharks called *Blue Water, White Death*.

Once aboard their dive boat on Dangerous Reef, Rodney mixed up a secret recipe of blood, horsemeat, and fish parts. Andrew ladled this "chum" from a large tub into the water, leaving a trail of smells that called to the sharks like a dinner bell.

Andrew Fox making chum

FACT:

Great whites have a keen sense of smell. They can detect even one drop of blood in 10 billion drops of water.

As the photographers pulled on their scuba tanks, the boat's crew finished tying tuna heads to the sides of the shark cages. The divers stepped from the boat into three large cages floating at the surface. Then the crew let out the lines so the cages would drift away from the boat, allowing the divers to watch for sharks from every direction.

They watched.

And waited.

Sometimes they waited in the boat, sometimes in the water. Jeff says, "Much of wildlife photography is waiting."

"A cage is a must when diving with great white sharks," Jeff says. "Being in a shark cage reverses the whole zoo experience. You become the animal behind the bars."

After about five hours, they saw a shape appear 50 to 60 feet (15 to 18 m) away. Jeff immediately realized that this was different from any other shark he'd ever seen. It did not move cautiously. It came straight toward them at a steady pace. As it got nearer, they realized how enormous it was. It yanked a tuna head off the side of the cage and vanished.

Hearts beating fast, the divers stared in the direction the shark had disappeared. For what seemed like a very long 15 minutes, nothing happened. Then the shark barreled into the other side of the cage and grabbed another tuna.

Jeff had just witnessed how great white sharks attack their prey. They sneak up from below and behind to ambush their victims in surprise attacks.

FACT:

Sample biting is how scientists describe the feeding behavior of great white sharks. They take a sample, and if it's good, they come back for more.

53

The next morning five great white sharks circled the cages. What an experience! Jeff knew that many divers never get to see one great white, let alone five.

Over the next 10 days, the divers spent many hours watching the sharks feed and snapping photos. Every day it was the same pattern. The largest shark would come to the cage first to feed on tuna heads, while the others waited 50 to 70 feet (15 to 21 m) away. Once the first left, the next largest shark would approach, following a pecking order.

From sunup to sundown, the divers would go into the cages for an hour and a half, come out for an hour, and go back in for two hours. After so many hours standing in 55°F (12.8°C) water, the divers never warmed up, even after they got back on the boat. Each day they had to add more layers to their wetsuits.

Jeff recalls his impressions of his first meeting with great whites. *"I was stunned by their size and power and how differently they behaved from other sharks. With most other sharks, I could imagine defending myself from an attack. With a white, I quickly realized that if this shark decides you are lunch, there is really nothing you can do about it."*

"When photographing great white sharks, never stick your hand or head outside the cage," advises Jeff. "That may seem obvious, but I have seen professionals do it. You may think there is only one shark out there, but other sharks could be lurking. And they have a knack for approaching on your blind side. Some photographers are so focused on filming the shark that they forget that one good chomp could be the end of their career!"

FACT:

Great white sharks have about 25 triangular teeth arranged in several rows. Like saw blades, their teeth easily slice off huge hunks of flesh. Some shark experts can identify the kind of shark just by its teeth, or even by the wounds the teeth leave in a shark attack victim.

HYPNOTIZING SHARKS
DYER ISLAND, SOUTH AFRICA

Jeff heard about another shark buff who seemed to be able to make sharks obey his command. Jeff had to see this for himself, so he went to Gansbaai, South Africa, to visit Andre Hartman, known as the shark wrangler.

Andre is a former spearfishing champion of South Africa. During one contest Andre was swimming back to the boat with his catch when a great white shark tried to make Andre *his* prize. Andre pushed the shark away with his spear gun, and the shark fled.

Another time, Andre was working on his dive boat when a great white tried to bite the outboard motor. Worried that the

Andre Hartman (far left) has a way with great whites.

56

shark would hurt his boat (and itself), Andre reached over the side to push the shark away. As he touched its snout with his hand, the shark suddenly leapt out of the water and opened its mouth as if to snap Andre up. But instead of trying to bite Andre, the shark slid harmlessly back into the sea.

Andre figured that he had accidentally overloaded the shark's sensory organs that detect the electricity generated by its surroundings. It was as if he'd put the shark into a trance. Andre repeated this feat with many other great white sharks and became famous for it.

FACT:

A shark has a special sense contained in pores along its jaw and snout called ampullae of Lorenzini. It detects the electrical field that radiates from every living thing (and many metallic objects).

When Jeff arrived in South Africa, Andre explained that the weather, wind, and water conditions had to be just right in order for Jeff to capture the image of the "hypnotized shark." For the next four weeks, as Jeff waited for the perfect day, he interviewed people with knowledge of great whites, photographed other sea life of the region, and read lots of books.

Finally, on the last day of Jeff's trip, the sea was calm. Andre exclaimed, "It's time!" They sped off in his motorboat to Dyer Island.

Andre stood on a step at the back of the boat and tossed out a shark liver tied to a rope. On cue a great white leaped to grab the bait. Andre reached over and touched its nose. The shark opened its mouth as wide as a patient in the dentist's chair.

"After 31 days of waiting, the shot took only 3 or 4 minutes," says Jeff. "Sometimes you have to wait a long time to get that one great photograph."

AIR JAWS
SEAL ISLAND, SOUTH AFRICA

Jeff wanted to investigate another amazing great white shark behavior he'd heard about at False Bay, South Africa. He met up with ocean guides Chris and Monique Fallows. Chris and a friend had discovered that great white sharks can breach like whales, jumping right out of the water to capture fur seals.

Jeff visited at the time of year when Cape fur seals give birth on nearby Seal Island, because that's when the great whites come for the seal meals. They hunt there until the pups and their parents leave.

In order to get to their feeding grounds, the seals have to get past the sharks lurking just beyond the shoreline. In groups of five to 20, the adult and young seals leap into the water from a rocky ledge that locals call The Launch Pad. They make a mad dash for their feeding grounds outside the bay, relying on safety in numbers. After a few days feeding at sea, they return to shore. It's on the return trip to the island, when seals are swimming back alone or in small groups, that the danger is greatest. On average, the seal colony loses seven seals a day to hungry sharks.

Where there is a colony of fur seals and their pups, you can be sure great whites are nearby.

More than half the successful attacks on seals happen around sunrise. From below, the sharks can see the seals against the brightening sky, but the seals have a hard time making out the dark back of a great white shark swimming below them. To catch a seal, a great white explodes out of the water in a burst of speed scientists estimate at about 20 miles (32 km) an hour.

Sometimes they jump as high as 10 feet (3 m) into the air.

The shark attacks its prey with a wide-open mouth that watchers call "Air Jaws." But if the shark misses on its first try, the seal just might get away. It may leap right over the head of the shark, escaping the giant jaws by inches. However the chase ends, it is sure to be a fur-raising experience for the seal.

A Cape fur seal narrowly escapes a great white.

A great "white" shark is really only white underneath. Its back is darker gray. This pattern is called countershading.

A great white shark is one of the only sharks that can leap out of the water in pursuit of prey.

About 60,000 Cape fur seals live on Seal Island during the pupping season, so it would seem that Jeff would have many chances to see a seal-shark encounter. But most of the hunting takes place underwater, which is not a safe place to be without a cage.

So the Fallows have devised a way to get sharks to jump on cue. They construct a seal decoy, which they tow behind a boat to tempt a great white to leap up and grab it. The Fallows have been successful in getting great white sharks to perform this action hundreds of times. Of course, they have to replace their decoy seals often.

Since 1996 the Fallows have been leading ecotourism trips to give visitors a chance to witness the amazing athletic behavior of great white sharks. They also collaborate on many research projects that help scientists learn more about shark behavior. And of course they give photographers such as Jeff the opportunity to catch a shark midair.

A great white breaches to attack a seal decoy.

A GREAT WHITE BUFFET
GUADALUPE ISLAND, MEXICO

In a place where tasty elephant seals, fur seals, and sea lions all gather to have their pups, great white sharks won't be far behind. From August through early December, tourists and underwater photographers are almost sure to find great white sharks lurking in the waters near Guadalupe Island off the coast of Mexico.

Jeff found that the great white sharks there are not as big as the ones he photographed in Australia. Most are about 11 feet (3.4 m) long, instead of 18 feet (5.5 m). But they are plenty big enough for the tourists who view them from cages suspended from dive boats.

Jeff explains that the bars of an aluminum cage won't prevent a great white from tearing it apart. Instead, the shark's electric sense detects a boundary that the shark usually won't cross. But there are exceptions. On rare occasions a shark gets so excited that it rushes at the cage. If a great white gets stuck between the bars of the cage, it panics and thrashes around as the divers cower in the corner. The shark tears apart the cage to free itself. All escape and the tourists go home with an amazing story of how they spent their vacation!

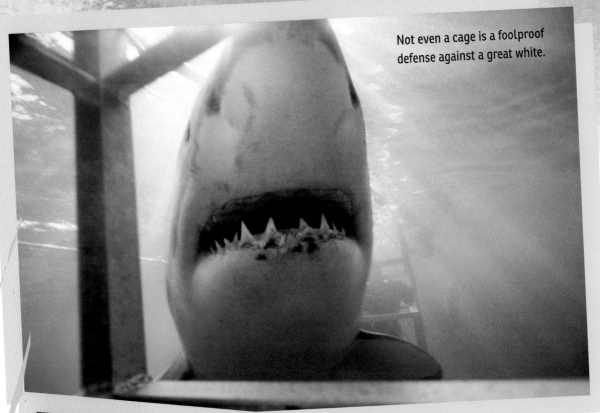

Not even a cage is a foolproof defense against a great white.

During his trip to Guadalupe Island, Jeff wanted to learn how far great whites would travel in search of food. Those are questions that shark scientists want to answer too. To learn about shark migration, they attach electronic tags to the dorsal fins of great whites. The tags send information from the sharks up to satellites circling Earth and back down to the researchers' labs. Information about where the sharks go and how deep they dive is relayed to computers. One great white traveled 12,000 miles (19,000 km) from South Africa to Australia and back in nine months.

The electronic tags show that many great white sharks swim out to the middle of the Pacific Ocean to an area that scientists have named the White Shark Café. The café is visited by great whites from Guadalupe, Mexico, and from along the northern California coast, around the Farallon Islands and Año Nuevo. They stay there for about three months, hunting squid, swordfish, and other sharks.

Experts aren't sure what draws the great whites all the way to the café. But the food there must make the long trip worthwhile; scientists who have tracked great white sharks from Guadalupe and back report that they return home looking well fed.

A satellite tag reveals to scientists that great white sharks travel thousands of miles each year.

68

FACT:

Generally great whites feed near the surface during the daytime. But they often dive much deeper, likely in search of prey. Satellite tags have shown that great whites may dive as deep as 4,000 feet (1,200 m).

HOW PEOPLE FEEL ABOUT GREAT WHITES

For years after the movie *Jaws* came out, many people refused to go swimming in the ocean because they were afraid they might run into a great white shark. In some seaside communities where there had never been a shark attack, police had to patrol the beaches to reassure swimmers that it was safe to go into the water. Great whites were stalked by big-game trophy hunters. Their teeth, jaws, and preserved bodies were valuable prizes.

Now concern for great whites is growing, and many people want to get as close as they can to great whites. But the sharks are getting harder to find. Even though great whites aren't caught for food, as many other sharks are, they still are hunted for sport in some places. Others are caught by accident in fishing nets. Great whites are listed as a "vulnerable" species, meaning that declining populations in many parts of the world are bringing them closer to extinction. Many countries now have laws to protect great whites and help increase their populations worldwide.

Shark teeth jewelry shows how variable shark teeth can be.

THE LEGACY OF *JAWS*

In 1975 a blockbuster movie called *Jaws* played in theaters. It was about a great white shark attacking swimmers at a popular beach. The movie scared people so much that there was a rush to kill great whites (and any other sharks). Stories of attacks still make the news and cause fear, but the odds of being eaten by a shark are extremely rare. You have an equal chance of being killed by falling airplane parts.

About 100 shark attacks are reported worldwide each year. A third to a half of those are blamed on great whites. You might think that all great white shark attacks would be fatal, but most are not. After a sample bite, great whites usually release humans. But that first nibble can cause serious damage.

Shark conservationists like Rodney and Andrew Fox, Andre Hartman, and Chris and Monique Fallows are calling for more laws to protect great whites. These people work around sharks on a daily basis and have a great respect for these top predators. They are working to set aside more areas of the ocean as marine sanctuaries. They are encouraging more ecotourism in order to fund the sanctuaries and to help the public understand great whites.

Underwater photographer Jeff Rotman is surrounded by the tools of his trade.

Whenever there is an attack on a human by a great white shark, some people call for changes in laws to allow great whites to be hunted. Jeff Rotman feels differently. "You have to share the ocean with these animals," he says. "You do take a risk in some areas of the ocean. But you won't fix that by killing every great white shark."

After all, we're visitors in their world. And Jeff will keep visiting and photographing their world to share its wonders with those of us above sea level.

THE LARGEST OF THEM ALL
WHALE SHARKS

If you know just one thing about whale sharks, it's probably this: The whale shark is the biggest fish in the world, but it eats some of the smallest animals in the ocean.

But did you know that the huge beast is perhaps the gentlest shark of all? At least that's what underwater photographer Jeff Rotman says. He calls the whale shark the friendliest shark in the sea.

In the ocean BIG doesn't always mean SCARY. (Of course, sometimes it does.)

A whale shark plays with a golden trevally fish on Ningaloo Reef in Australia.

Jeff has been fascinated with sharks for years. From the tiny pygmy shark to the granddaddy of them all—the whale shark—Jeff loves discovering new things about sharks, rays, and other shark relatives.

WHALE SHARK STATS

AVERAGE LENGTH
32 feet (9.8 meters)

MAXIMUM LENGTH
45 feet (13.7 m)— like most sharks, females are larger than males

MAXIMUM WEIGHT
more than 15 tons (13.6 metric tons)

RANGE
worldwide in temperate and tropical seas

LIFE SPAN
100 years or more

DIET
plankton, krill, squid, and small fish

"What impresses me most about the incredible variety of sharks is how well each species is adapted to live in different parts of the world's oceans and feed on so many different kinds of prey," says Jeff. "The biggest sharks defy the popular image of sharks as fearsome predators with row upon row of sharp teeth. Whale sharks, basking sharks, and manta rays are not at all aggressive, despite the fact that they are the biggest fishes in the ocean."

AUSTRALIA IS A GREAT PLACE TO DINE

Diver Rodney Fox is Australia's most outspoken defender of sharks. He was the one who first introduced Jeff to great whites. Rodney saw that Jeff shared his passion for sharks, so he invited him to meet the whale sharks of Australia's Ningaloo Reef.

April and May are a perfect time to spot whale sharks there. Cold currents rise up from the deep ocean off the west coast of Australia. They provide the fertilizer that makes tiny plants called phytoplankton bloom. Phytoplankton feed swarms of tiny animals called zooplankton, which in turn feed larger animals, such as squid and small fish. Any of these could soon find themselves in the belly of a whale shark. And, if lucky, a shark photographer could find himself or herself with a great close-up of the biggest shark in the world.

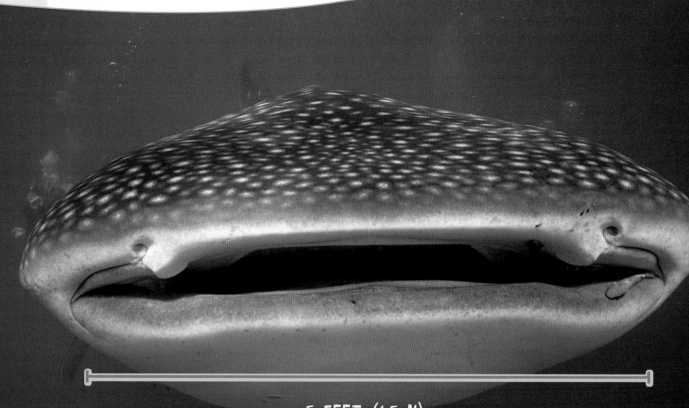

5 FEET (1.5 M)

NINGALOO REEF

Ningaloo Reef extends for 160 miles (257 kilometers) along the coast of western Australia. In some places the fringing reef is so close to shore that snorkelers and divers can step off the beach and soon be swimming among hundreds of kinds of colorful reef fish, corals, and shellfish.

hawksbill turtle

In addition to whale sharks, manta rays, humpback whales, dolphins, and dugongs make Ningaloo Marine Park their winter retreat. And mother loggerhead, green, and hawksbill turtles clamber onto its beaches to lay their eggs.

Indian Ocean

AUSTRALIA

NINGALOO

FACT:

It might be terrifying to face a whale shark underwater, but humans have nothing to fear. Scientists don't believe whale sharks use their teeth to bite or chew. And even if you did somehow fall into a whale shark's nearly 5-foot- (1.5-m-) wide mouth, it would simply spit you back out. Plankton and small fish don't have a chance, but humans aren't on a whale shark's menu.

Like basking sharks and the deep-sea megamouth sharks, the whale shark is a filter feeder. It swims forward, mouth wide open, to ram water and food into its gigantic mouth. (Its width is about the height of an average 9-year-old!)

Along with the water come tiny snacks, including fish eggs, shrimp, and krill. The water is flushed back out, but the bits of food are forced up to the roof of the mouth, where they get stuck in a mucous covering. The whale shark gulps, and down go the plankton and other goodies.

A whale shark's waking hours are spent swimming and eating, eating and swimming. But every so often, it stops feeding and does what's best described as a whale shark version of a cough. You wouldn't want to be on the receiving end of that. Scientists think it is how the sharks clean trapped food particles off mouthparts called gill rakers. Wouldn't it be handy to just cough instead of brushing your teeth?

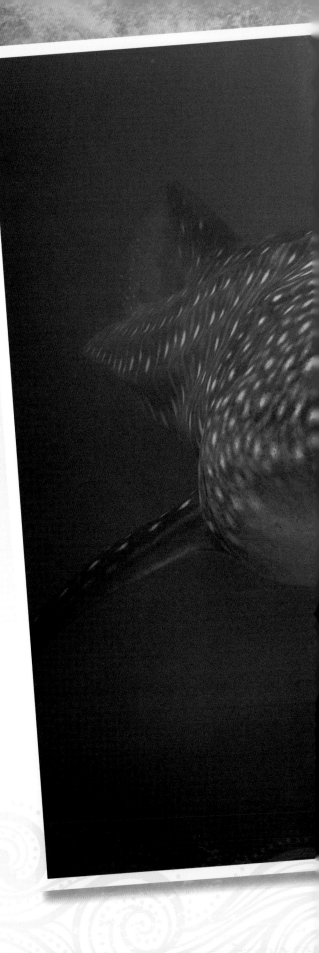

pelagic squid

FACT:

Though primarily filter feeders, whale sharks also capture larger prey such as squid, sardines, and anchovies.

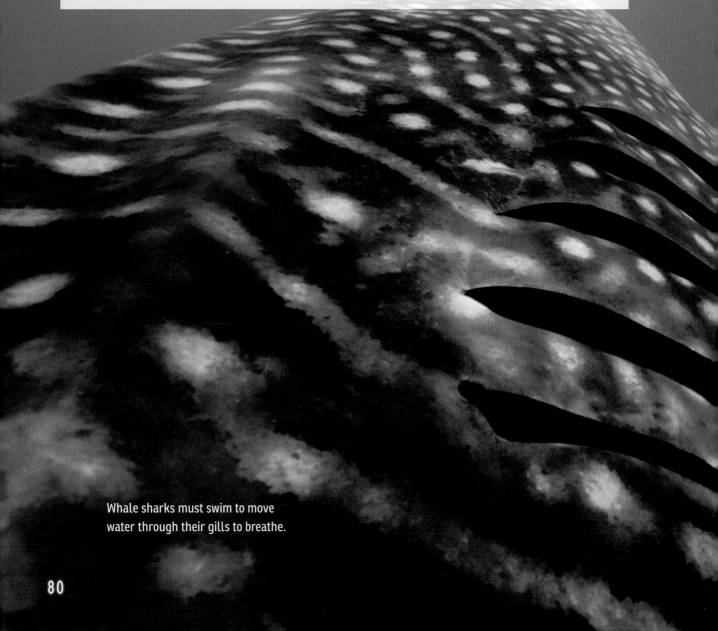

THE HUNT IS ON

Jeff was ready to meet the whale sharks. But he and Rodney Fox needed help to find them. To discover where they were feeding, a spotter plane flew over Ningaloo Reef each day to scout the sharks' location.

On the fourth day of searching, the pilot spotted whale sharks where the coral reef drops off sharply into deep water. He radioed the divers, who then headed their boat toward the action.

Whale sharks must swim to move water through their gills to breathe.

Jeff and Rodney strapped on their gear and tumbled backward off the side of the boat. They peered in the direction the spotter had instructed. Success!

At 20 feet (6 m) below the surface, a ghostly image appeared in the distance. Jeff watched in amazement as an enormous, gaping mouth came steadily toward him. The huge whale shark seemed unaware that Jeff was in its path. Just when it seemed as if it might swallow him up, the shark dipped down and swam under him. Jeff found himself staring down at the giant gray back passing beneath him, beautifully mottled with pale yellow stripes and spots.

WHY DO DIVERS FALL BACKWARD OFF A BOAT?

Beginning divers are usually taught to sit on the rail of a small boat and fall backward into the water as they hold onto their face masks. This way the dive masks stay in place and the heavy dive tanks don't land on top of them. If a diver fell face first into the water, he or she might hit the side of the boat—a tough way to start an underwater adventure. Another option is the giant stride, for a diver who wants to just step off into the blue. But it's called the giant stride for a reason—if you don't jump far enough out, your tank will hit the side of the boat.

Some divers take a giant stride to enter the water.

Jeff had never been close to a whale shark before. "Nothing prepares you to meet an animal of this size underwater," said Jeff. "It's a different kind of 'large' altogether from a great white shark. A great white is the size of a family car. The whale shark is a school bus. Plus, objects underwater look bigger than they actually are, which made it seem humongous!"

Fifteen to 20 remoras swam along beneath the white belly of the whale shark. They know a good thing when they see it. Also called suckerfish, remoras stick to whale sharks using suction cups on their heads, grabbing scraps of food from their host as they are carried along. And who would attack a remora under the shelter of such a huge protector?

Jeff was so intent on capturing photographs that he lost all fear of the huge animal. The whale shark went by him so slowly that he couldn't resist grabbing onto its dorsal fin as it passed. Holding on with one hand, Jeff kept shooting pictures with the other. As he was dragged through the water, he got close-up shots of its mouth, eyes, gills, and the spots that identify each individual whale shark.

Remoras stick to the belly of a whale shark.

FACT:

The whale shark's skin is very thick—4 inches (10 centimeters) or more. Skin this thick can resist the bites of all but great whites and a few other fierce predators. The yellow-white stripes and spots that cover the shark's back help it blend in among shafts of sunlight reaching into the water, giving the enormous fish a bit of camouflage as it hunts.

Jeff's whale shark taxi started to dive very slowly and gently. As he went deeper and deeper, Jeff had to keep swallowing to clear his ears to equalize the pressure. Meanwhile, the whale shark continued its lazy journey downward, sometimes actively swimming, sometimes gliding, in search of food.

After a few minutes, Jeff noticed that the light around him was fading. He looked at his depth gauge. He was 130 feet (39.6 m) below the surface. But still he held onto the fin. Then, as if it was getting tired of its hitchhiker, the whale shark sped up and began to dive more steeply. Finally, Jeff had to let go.

It was only then that he realized he was running out of air and that his ears were aching from the intense pressure. He kicked for the surface as quickly as he could, but he had to stop often to give his body time to adjust to the changing water pressure.

THE BENDS

Why couldn't Jeff just rocket for the surface as fast as possible? He had to make sure that he didn't get a very serious condition that doctors call decompression sickness and divers call the bends.

Think of what happens when you unscrew the cap on a bottle of soda. The gas that was dissolved in the liquid at high pressure comes out as bubbles when the pressure is released.

Scuba divers breathe compressed gases from their air tanks. If a diver rises too quickly, bubbles of gas can form in the bloodstream and move around the body, especially to shoulders, elbows, knees, and ankles. The bubbles can cause intense pain and potentially even death.

"My amazement at this gentle giant made it easy to forget my number one safety rule: Never get too comfortable around a shark." says Jeff. "Had the shark decided to give me a slap with its enormous tail, it would have knocked me into the next ocean—or at least unconscious!"

A HOME FOR WHALE SHARKS

Whale sharks can grow to be about 45 feet (13.7 m) long. Their size makes them way too big to be kept in most aquariums. One place that has been able to house whale sharks is the Churaumi Aquarium in Okinawa, Japan. Several whale sharks swim with manta rays, yellowfin tuna, and other big fish inside a tank that holds nearly 2 million gallons (7,500 cubic meters) of seawater. That's enough water to fill about 50,000 bathtubs.

In the ocean you may find whale sharks in tropical seas, like those around Australia, as well as in the warm waters off Mexico and Asia. At one time there was a market for whale shark meat in Asia. Today whale sharks are protected from fishing.

SHY SHARK
BASKING SHARKS

A whale shark is curious and approachable. A basking shark—another giant—is the exact opposite. Perhaps it comes from living in cold, murky water, where it barely can see any of its neighbors through the gloom. This giant shark is used to traveling alone or in small groups. It does not seem to welcome human companions like Jeff who want to swim alongside it.

The basking shark plows through the water with its mouth open, catching zooplankton and small fish on its gill rakers. Filter feeding must work well for it, because a basking shark can grow to about 33 feet (10 m), making it the world's second largest fish after the whale shark.

A basking shark opens its mouth wide to catch plankton.

The first time Jeff tried to get close enough to a basking shark to take its picture was one summer in the Irish Sea. In July huge blooms of phytoplankton turn the waters off the Isle of Man into a pea-green sea soup. "The water here between Scotland and Wales is freezing cold, even in summer, and the weather is always rainy and foggy," Jeff recalled. But that makes it a perfect spot to look for basking sharks.

ISLE OF MAN

SCOTLAND

NORTHERN IRELAND

IRELAND

ENGLAND

WALES

BASKING SHARK STATS

AVERAGE LENGTH
22 feet (6.7 m)

RANGE
temperate coastal waters

MAXIMUM LENGTH
33 feet (10 m)

LIFE SPAN
50 years

MAXIMUM WEIGHT
4 tons (3.6 metric tons)

DIET
plankton, krill, and jellyfish

Scientists estimate that a large
basking shark can filter nearly
400,000 gallons (1,500 cubic meters)
of water per hour.

HIDE AND SEEK

Day after day Jeff waited and watched, hoping to see a giant dorsal fin peek above the water. The basking shark likely got its name from its habit of cruising near the surface. To early shark watchers, it may have appeared that the sharks were basking in the sun like sunbathers. But they were most likely feeding on plankton, which tend to drift on ocean currents near the surface.

That behavior made basking sharks easy for fishermen to catch. They were almost hunted to extinction, but now basking sharks and whale sharks are protected by international agreement.

Jeff knew that basking sharks are shy and easily frightened. He also knew that the bubbles and the gurgling sounds from a scuba tank could scare them away, so he had to plan his dives carefully. To be as quiet as possible, he used a mask and snorkel instead of a tank, which meant he would have to hold his breath for as long as he could. "We even put Vaseline on the rubber straps of our flippers so they wouldn't squeak against our heels," he said, "because as soon as the shark senses that you are there, it disappears."

The basking sharks would flee if they heard a boat engine. Instead the divers quietly rowed an inflatable rubber raft out to the area where the basking sharks fed. When they got close, Jeff slipped silently into the water. He took a big gulp of air and dove down into the cold, gray-green water. The plankton was so thick he couldn't see very far in any direction.

In fact, the water was so murky and the light so dim that Jeff didn't see the basking shark at all—until it was right on top of him. Startled, Jeff snapped as many photographs as he could before the animal retreated into the gloom like a ghost disappearing into the mist.

IF AT FIRST YOU DON'T SUCCEED ...

Not every expedition is a success. "I spent two weeks trying to get a good photograph," Jeff said. "Unfortunately, I wasn't happy with any of my pictures. So I returned the next year—on my honeymoon!"

It might not have been the type of honeymoon that anyone but a diver would dream of, but after two more weeks on the Isle of Man, Jeff finally got the photos he wanted.

BLUE WATER SURPRISE
GIANT MANTA RAYS

Did you ever discover something you never expected to find that was even better than what you were actually looking for? That's what happened to Jeff during an expedition with divers hunting supersized swordfish and tuna.

Jeff met up with the group, called Blue Water Hunters, in the Socorro Islands, about 250 miles (400 km) south of Mexico's Baja California. Each member of the group is a champion free diving underwater hunter. They spend more than eight hours a day in the water, diving down 80 to 100 feet (24 to 30 m) without scuba gear, for a chance to catch a giant "trophy" fish using only a spear gun.

The diving group did find some really big fish on that expedition, but not the ones they were expecting. Instead they found what a scientist has described as "small cars with wings."

A Blue Water Hunter catches a giant wahoo, one of the fastest fish in the ocean.

UNITED STATES

MEXICO

SOCORRO ISLANDS

94

Some giant mantas have a "wingspan" of nearly 30 feet (9 m).

Jeff's plan was to take photographs of the Blue Water Hunters swimming in the open sea. "A Blue Water Hunter is the closest thing to a man-fish," Jeff says. They have trained themselves to slow their heart rates so that they can hold their breath for minutes at a time.

Their boat steamed out to an area of the Pacific Ocean that was a deep, dark blue, a sign that the water there was thousands of feet deep. The hunters jumped overboard as gleefully as kids diving into a swimming pool.

Even though Jeff is an expert diver, he admitted that diving in the open ocean with miles of water beneath you can be a bit scary. But in he went with the Blue Water Hunters.

Jeff was shooting photographs of the hunters as they made dive after dive, when suddenly one, then two, then six giant manta rays swarmed around them. The hunters forgot their quest for giant tuna and wahoo. They swam back to the boat to trade their spear guns for underwater cameras.

GIANT MANTA RAY STATS

AVERAGE WIDTH
17 to 22 feet (5 to 6.7 m)

LIFE SPAN
up to 40 years

MAXIMUM WIDTH
29.5 feet (9 m)

DIET
plankton, krill, and jellyfish

MAXIMUM WEIGHT
about 3 tons (2.7 metric tons)

NICKNAME
devilfish

RANGE
tropical and temperate oceans

A MOST UNUSUAL SKELETON

Rays and sharks are close relatives. Unlike most other fish, which have hard, bony skeletons like ours, sharks and rays have skeletons made of cartilage. That is the same flexible material you have in your ears and the tip of your nose. Cartilage in the fins of the manta ray gives it the flexibility and support it needs to "fly" gracefully through the water.

The noodlelike strands of cartilage are also what make sharks so highly prized for use in shark fin soup. Each year about 40 million sharks are caught just for their fins.

A giant ray gives a ride to a remora—and to the diver holding onto the remora's tail.

Remoras attach themselves to giant
rays as well as whale sharks and others,
seeking protection and free food.

Forgetting about their fishing trip, the hunters played with the mantas for hours each day. Often the rays would roll over like puppies. Black splotches on their white bellies helped the divers identify individual rays. Remoras hitchhiked anywhere they could attach themselves to the giant fish.

Sometimes a manta ray would float just a few feet above the head of a diver, so close that the diver could have reached up and scratched its belly. Some scientists think this is the same behavior that the manta rays display at cleaning stations. Perhaps the rays thought the divers were there to clean them.

AT THE CAR WASH

Cleaning stations are where sea animals gather to have small cleaner fish pick off parasites that irritate their skin, mouth, and gills. When a manta ray stops and hovers like a helicopter, it is a signal to the cleaner that the ray is not planning to eat it. It's waiting its turn to be cleaned. After the cleaners nibble parasites off the ray's body, they may turn their attention to the remoras that accompany the manta and help them out as well.

Blue Water Hunter Terry Maas hitches
a ride on a giant manta ray.

THE DEVILFISH ROLLER COASTER

That day at the Socorro Islands, champion American free diver Terry Maas dove to about 35 feet (10.7 m). There a manta ray came up to Terry, slowed down, and looked right at him. Terry saw it as an invitation. He grabbed onto the manta ray's scaly head and draped himself across the big fish's back. Terry got the ride of his life.

The manta ray gently flapped its "wings," which are overgrown pectoral fins. The ray made graceful loops, like a slow-motion roller coaster. After about three minutes, Terry had to return to the surface to take a breath. When he dove back down, the manta ray was waiting for him. Again and again, the ride continued after Terry returned from gulping a lungful of air. It was as if the manta ray was a taxi waiting for its passenger.

Manta rays don't have stingers on their tails like their stingray relatives.

A manta ray has small fins that resemble horns on either side of its head to herd zooplankton, such as copepods, shrimp, and newly hatched fish, into its mouth. The fins started out as side fins. While the baby manta ray was still growing inside its mother, pieces of the side fins separated to become head fins. (Scientists call them cephalic fins.) When it is swimming fast, a manta ray can curl up the fins to make itself more streamlined.

The helpful fins may be the reason that the manta ray was once called devilfish—they reminded people of a devil's horns. Another legend that may have made people fearful of manta rays was based on their ability to leap out of the water. Some tales claim that mantas would jump onto small boats to crush sailors. (It may have happened—by accident.) It is more likely that mantas breach like whales to scrape parasites off their skin as they slap the water coming back down.

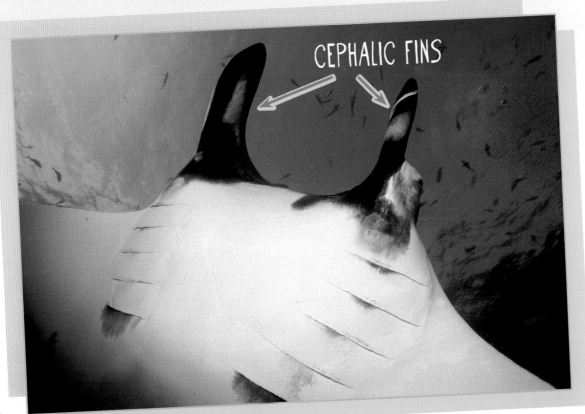

CEPHALIC FINS

THE FUTURE FOR GIANTS

Some mantas are accidentally caught in fishing nets. Others are hunted outright. Jeff believes manta rays need to be better protected from humans who pursue them.

Many manta rays are caught for food and for their gills, which are used to make Asian medicines. Patients are told that the gills of these fish filter out particles from seawater, so the gills should help filter out diseases or poisons from the human body. But there is no scientific evidence that this is true.

Guy Stevens, founder and director of the Manta Trust, helped convince representatives from 178 countries to vote to protect mantas. Mantas were added to a list of protected plants and animals under international rules in March 2013. This action can help control the trade in manta ray gills.

a manta ray caught in a fishing net

Giant fish like the whale shark are now protected by international agreement.

Guy says that there is another important thing that may help protect manta rays—us! Tourists such as scuba divers and snorkelers spend more than $140 million a year to visit tropical waters in Mexico, Fiji, Indonesia, Sri Lanka, and India, where mantas and tourists can swim together. Some of that money goes to programs that help protect ocean habitats and preserve them for the future.

Whale sharks, basking sharks, and manta rays are listed as protected animals by CITES—the Convention on International Trade in Endangered Species. It is proof that the world is beginning to appreciate the gentle giants and their place in the sea.

COCOS ISLAND

The diver plunged into the ocean, kicked his long swim fins, and headed straight down the side of the jagged cliff of an extinct volcano. He passed by a colorful school of fairy basslets. A spiny lobster peeked out from its hiding place in the black rock.

At 100 to 130 feet (30 to 40 meters), where the sunlight is only a distant glow, underwater photographer Jeff Rotman spotted his prey. He dove even deeper to get underneath the school of fish for the best shot of the giant creatures. Jeff raised his camera and clicked photo after photo before the 100 scalloped hammerhead sharks dispersed in fright, terrified by the flash of his camera.

Jeff had come thousands of miles to Cocos Island to get just this image.

Scalloped hammerheads have a distinctive shape that makes them instantly recognizable.

Costa Rica's Cocos Island is a tiny volcanic island in the Pacific Ocean, far from any place inhabited by humans. Over the years Jeff has visited Cocos Island many times. He has seen firsthand that many of the shark species that were once plentiful there have all but disappeared because of overfishing. Now Jeff comes not just to photograph the sharks, but also to document the dangers that threaten them. He hopes his photos can show why it's so important to protect the top predators of the ocean.

SHARK CENTRAL

To underwater explorers like Jeff, Cocos Island is known as the Island of the Sharks. In addition to sea turtles, whales, and dolphins, the waters surrounding Cocos Island have manta rays, tiger sharks, hammerhead sharks, whale sharks, and many more kinds of sharks rarely seen in other places—and never in the huge numbers found here. "Cocos Island is the single best place on the planet to see a variety of sharks," Jeff says.

But Cocos Island isn't easy to get to. It's more than 300 miles (500 kilometers) off the coast of Central America. Jeff travels on the dive boat *Sea Hunter* out of Costa Rica. It takes 45 hours of bouncing over rough seas to reach the island.

The island and the waters for 9 miles (15 km) around it make up the Cocos Island National Park. The park has rules for visitors; for example, only three boats have permission to take divers to visit the underwater park, and only the park ranger may stay overnight on Cocos Island. So the 90-foot- (27-m-) long dive boat is Jeff's home for the next 30 days.

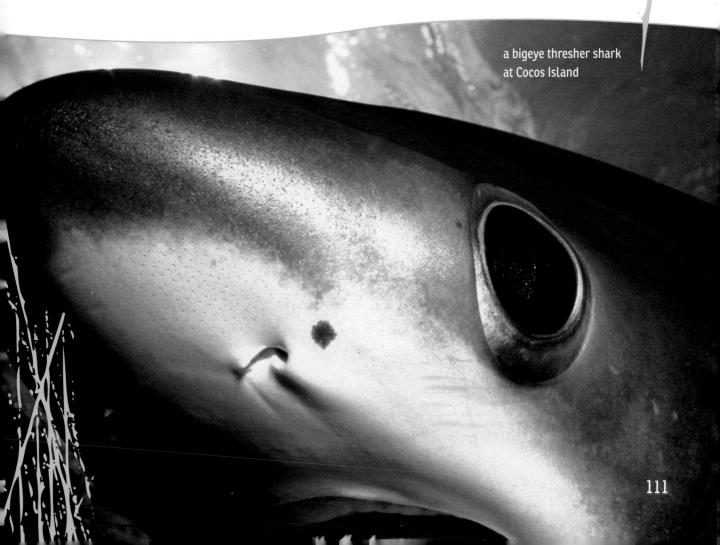

AT SEA ON *SEA HUNTER*

The *Sea Hunter* is not luxurious. It is a workboat that was formerly a scientific research vessel. Divers share cramped quarters with four bunks in each cabin. Most of the rest of the space is filled with scuba tanks and other diving equipment, storage lockers, and workstations for doing research or viewing film footage.

a bigeye thresher shark at Cocos Island

So what is it about Cocos Island that makes it Shark Central? Food, of course. You might say it's like a giant seafood buffet—an all-you-can-eat feast for sharks.

Several ocean currents swirl around the island. Where ocean currents converge, marine life gathers. Ocean currents are often called "ocean highways." They transport tiny plants and animals called plankton, which directly or indirectly feed almost everything else in the ocean.

Larger ocean creatures, such as turtles, whales, and fish, converge as they follow the currents or are swept up by them, until they reach the rich feeding grounds of Cocos Island. Scientists say there are about 300 different species of fish that live around Cocos Island. Wherever there are small fish, bigger ones, such as sharks, come too.

Many sharks also visit the area for another reason—the presence of many different kinds of cleaner fish. Big fish gather at cleaning stations on the coral reef to wait for the cleaners to work on them. Cleaner fish perform a useful service by plucking annoying parasites off the skin, gills, and jaws of the larger fish. The sharks get cleaned, and the little cleaners get a meal.

A trumpetfish hides among a school of blue-striped snappers.

STAYING SAFE IN STRONG CURRENTS

Exploring the deep, treacherous waters of Cocos Island is only for experienced divers. The currents are so strong that they can carry divers far away from their dive boats. To make sure he isn't lost at sea, Jeff carries a long orange rubber tube that he can blow up should he get swept away by the current. In such circumstances, he'd wave it in the air so that the dive boat could find him. For night dives he packs a strobe light, like a bicycle rider might use. If needed, the flashing light would signal his location.

TRICKS OF THE TRADE

It's one thing to see a shark; it's quite another to shoot the perfect photograph of one. Jeff Rotman has learned many strategies to make the most of his dive expeditions.

1. FIND A SHARK.

This is the first challenge. Jeff has used high-tech tools including spotter planes to locate whale sharks. Other times his tools are as simple as a cut-out figure of a seal, like the duck decoys used by hunters. The seal silhouette prompted a great white shark to leap out of the water right next to Jeff—a dream shot for a shark photographer.

2. OFFER TREATS.

Food is a good way to introduce yourself to a shark or ray, says Jeff. Chum, a tasty mixture of horsemeat, blood, and fish oil, is a yummy draw for great whites. But be careful—too many treats can get your subject overexcited.

3. SAFETY FIRST.

No matter how eager he is to get his shot, Jeff always takes safety measures. Sometimes he wears a chainmail dive suit. That works for medium-sized sharks like Caribbean reef sharks, but only a strong shark cage provides enough protection when you are diving among great whites.

4. BRING A BUDDY.

Jeff always has another diver to watch his back—literally. He never dives anywhere without his safety diver and good friend, Asher Gal.

5. BE POLITE.

Jeff says that this is the most important rule of diving with sharks. You are a guest in their world. Don't chase, corner, or grab them. Let them come to you. Or, if you are Jeff, inch toward them very, very slowly.

tiger shark

Jeff shooting Caribbean reef sharks

THINKING LIKE A SHARK

Jeff's job begins long before he jumps into the water with his camera. Before any dive expedition, he does his homework, learning all he can about the kinds of sharks he may meet. He tries to understand and predict how they will behave around him.

Although Jeff has a checklist of the animals he hopes to photograph on his trips to Cocos Island, he is prepared for whatever shows up at this crossroads in the Pacific Ocean. He hopes to find schools of scalloped hammerheads, silky sharks, whitetip and silvertip sharks, and even dangerous tiger sharks. But swordfish, sailfish, tuna, whale sharks, Galápagos sharks, and many more large fish also come here, where nutritious tidbits are pushed up from the deep, supplying food for all.

When Jeff (right) and Asher Gal are working in remote areas like Cocos Island, they have to bring 10 to 12 different cameras and back-up gear for everything. There are no stores to resupply.

Jeff photographs Asher with a swordfish being illegally caught by fishermen. Jeff uses his photos to let the world know what is happening to the ocean's top predators.

HUNTING HAMMERHEADS

It's not hard to figure out how the hammerhead shark got its name—its head is shaped like a hammer. At either end of its flattened head sit its eyes and nostrils. A hammerhead swings its head from side to side as it swims. Having eyes at either end of that broad head may help it scan a wider area on the ocean floor as it searches for prey.

Around its nose, mouth, and jaws are many tiny pores called ampullae of Lorenzini. They are the source of the shark's amazing ability to detect the electricity given off by other animals, such as a stingray buried in the sand. Scientists say the shark uses its head to pin the stingray down before grasping it with razor-sharp teeth. Many hammerheads have a stingray spine embedded in their jaws to prove it.

With eyes on either side, a hammerhead has a head made for hunting.

SCALLOPED HAMMERHEAD STATS

AVERAGE LENGTH
10 to 12 feet (3 to 3.7 m)

MAXIMUM LENGTH
14 feet (4.3 m)

MAXIMUM WEIGHT
336 pounds (152 kilograms)

RANGE
tropical Atlantic and Pacific oceans

LIFE SPAN
more than 30 years

DIET
mostly fish, small stingrays, sardines,
mackerel, and herring

FACT:

Scalloped hammerheads can be huge and scary-looking, but they are actually rather shy around divers. Scalloped hammerheads are not dangerous man-eaters like the infamous great hammerhead.

Jeff waited hours to capture this shot of a scalloped hammerhead waiting its turn to be groomed at a cleaning station.

Jeff was on a mission to photograph hammerheads. The dive boat operators took him to a cove where scalloped hammerheads come to get groomed by cleaner fish. Jeff dove to a depth of about 100 feet (30 m) and squatted down on the ocean floor behind a big rock. For several minutes he sat motionless, his camera at the ready, making himself part of the landscape. Jeff's safety diver, Asher, stood guard a short distance away. They watched and waited for the hammerheads to arrive.

Their patience was rewarded when a giant school of 100 scalloped hammerheads swam past them. One turned off from the group and headed toward a big boulder where cleaner fish waited—and where Jeff was hiding. When the shark neared the cleaning station, it slowed almost to a standstill to let small cleaner fish called barberfish do their job. Jeff got several shots before the camera-shy hammerhead turned and fled.

"DEEPSEE" DIVING

To find scalloped hammerheads in deeper water, Jeff boarded the *DeepSee*, a submersible that can carry three people to a depth of 1,500 feet (450 m). *DeepSee*'s thick acrylic sphere provides a 360-degree view so it feels like you are actually swimming among the fish, even though you are at a depth that would crush a diver.

The crew descended along the steep slope of the extinct volcano. At 500 feet (150 m), it was so dark that the lights of the submersible didn't reach more than 25 feet (7.6 m). A scalloped hammerhead materialized out of the gloom and nearly crashed into the submersible. "It was a lovely surprise," remembers Jeff. "Being surprised is one of the things you can always count on at Cocos."

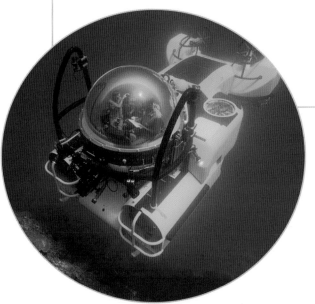

SILVERTIPS BY DAY

Other sharks congregated at various cleaning stations on the ocean floor. Jeff's dive guides showed him a shallow cove where every afternoon around 3:30 p.m. silvertip sharks come to a cleaning station staffed by fish called trevally jacks. Each day the sharks would stay for an hour or more before swimming off into the sunset. The divers had never heard of this behavior in silvertips.

For eight days the divers watched in amazement as young and old silvertips repeated the ritual of stopping at this spot to be cleaned. Usually four to seven sharks showed up, always in the late afternoon. One of the biggest silvertips, about 8 feet (2.5 m) long, had a ragged lower jaw, a clue that it had made a narrow escape from a fishhook.

Silvertips can be dangerous if divers meet them in the open ocean. But here they usually ignored Jeff, who could creep up within several feet of them to get some shots. If he came any closer, though, the adult sharks would charge and swerve away at the last minute. "I crossed an invisible line. It was a clear message to me to back off! But after all," admits Jeff, "this is their territory."

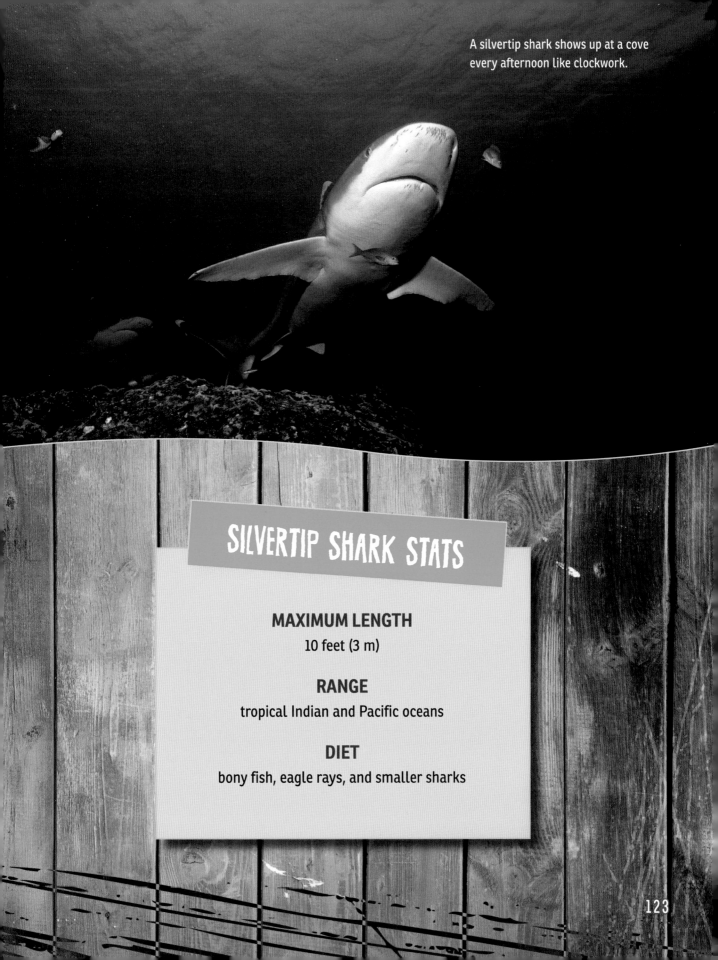

A silvertip shark shows up at a cove every afternoon like clockwork.

SILVERTIP SHARK STATS

MAXIMUM LENGTH
10 feet (3 m)

RANGE
tropical Indian and Pacific oceans

DIET
bony fish, eagle rays, and smaller sharks

WHITETIPS AT NIGHT

During the day Jeff explored shallow caves about 40 feet (12 m) below the surface, where many young whitetip reef sharks hang out, lounging on top of one another. At only 1.5 feet (46 cm) long, they hide in the rocks to avoid larger sharks that could easily gobble them up.

But the real adventure begins at night, when the adult whitetips go on the prowl. Like packs of wolves, they hunt and corner their prey. If one whitetip detects a sleeping parrotfish or surgeonfish inside a crack in the volcanic rock, the shark will try to force its snout into the hole to grab the fish. As the shark wriggles its whole body vigorously to try to reach the prey, its thrashing attracts as many as 50 other whitetips. They bombard the fish's hiding place until one of the sharks captures it. Then the other sharks often gang up on the winner to try to snatch its prize right out of its mouth.

FACT:

To make sure he disrupted the sharks' night behavior as little as possible, Jeff would let the batteries for his dive light run low during the day. Instead of a bright beam, it emitted only a faint glow, just enough for Jeff to find his way in the dark.

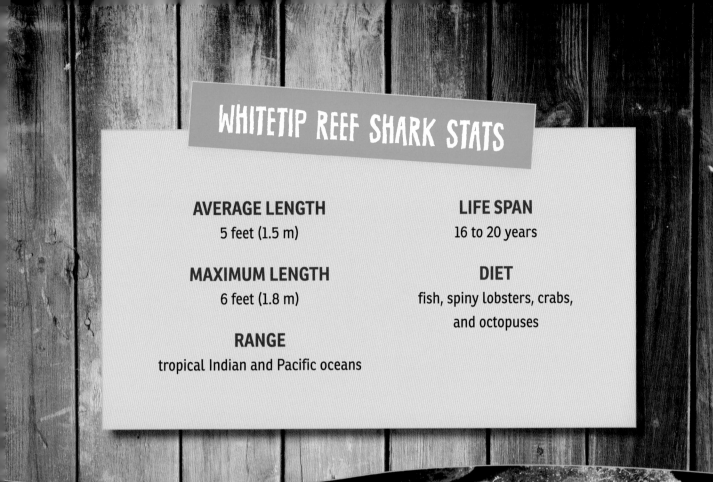

WHITETIP REEF SHARK STATS

AVERAGE LENGTH
5 feet (1.5 m)

LIFE SPAN
16 to 20 years

MAXIMUM LENGTH
6 feet (1.8 m)

DIET
fish, spiny lobsters, crabs,
and octopuses

RANGE
tropical Indian and Pacific oceans

Many whitetip reef sharks swarm
around rocks where they know
smaller fish are hiding.

TIGER SHARKS TAKE OVER

Scientists say the reason there are so many whitetip reef sharks at Cocos Island is that many larger sharks that would normally feed on the smaller sharks are gone—caught by fishermen. Without large predators, the population of whitetips has exploded.

Tiger sharks, famous for eating almost anything, have moved in to take advantage of the feast. The tiger sharks come into the shallow waters around Cocos Island at night to feed on whitetips, helping to reduce their population.

Sharks eat other sharks. Tiger sharks come to Cocos Island to feed on the smaller whitetip sharks.

TIGER TAMING

Like most sharks, a tiger shark is naturally curious about the funny, finned creatures that make lots of bubbles. Jeff's safety diver, Asher, carries a pole with three needlelike projections on one end. Just before a shark's curiosity prompts it to take a test bite, Asher gently taps the shark's snout with the pole. The shark quickly gets the message and backs off. Jeff says, "A test bite is one way that a shark can figure out if something is OK to eat. But I'd rather not be tested!"

Tiger sharks are among a handful of sharks that Jeff considers very dangerous. "I would never let a tiger shark out of my sight," he says. If he were attacked, as a last resort he would pull off his air tank and hold it in front of his chest to defend himself. So far, he has never had to.

TIGER SHARK STATS

AVERAGE LENGTH
12 to 14 feet (3.7 to 4.3 m)

RANGE
worldwide in warm seas

LIFE SPAN
40 to 50 years

DIET
marine mammals, marine reptiles, fish, lobsters, and squid

FACT:

Besides eating other sharks, tiger sharks feed on stingrays, seals, birds, and squid. Occasionally, they also munch on stranger fare. Car license plates, alarm clocks, bricks, bottles, and beer cans have been found inside the stomachs of tiger sharks, earning them the nickname "swimming trashcans."

SURROUNDED BY SILKY SHARKS

One way Jeff locates sharks is by watching what other animals do. Where lots of animals gather, you know there's something exciting going on.

Jeff really wanted to photograph a phenomenon called a bait ball, in which sharks feed mid-ocean on a huge school of fish. Bait balls occur when a school of fish is squeezed into a tight circle by predators both below and above. Sharks, dolphins, or tuna force the school to the surface, where seabirds join the attack from the air. It's a feeding frenzy photo opportunity. And it's a very, very dangerous place to be.

Jeff spent hours each day at Cocos scanning the horizon with his binoculars. He was on the lookout for seabirds shrieking and diving into the water. After six days of waiting, he saw a commotion not far away. Jeff and the dive team jumped into their inflatable boat and raced to the site where frigate birds and brown-footed boobies were gorging themselves. Some were already too heavy to fly. They paddled around weakly, their bellies stuffed with fish called green jacks.

bait ball

Diving birds signal action
just below the surface.

Jeff and Asher dove into the water about 200 feet (60 m) from the bait ball. It was already late afternoon, and the approaching sunset made it harder for the divers to see very far underwater. Within seconds, dozens of silky sharks swarmed around them. As the feeding continued, the sharks became more and more excited. Jeff tried to focus his camera as Asher stayed nearby with extra cameras at the ready.

The light was too dim for Jeff to get a good shot without using the flash on his camera. When he turned on his strobe light, the high-pitched whine of the battery made the sharks go wild. They began to ram the divers with their snouts. It felt like being punched in the stomach. Jeff and Asher looked at each other through their masks and were of the same mind: It was time to get out of there.

They kicked to the surface and flagged down the waiting boat. As they flopped into it, they agreed that there must be more than 100 silkies below them. It was only then that they could admire how the light had shimmered against the silky skin that these sharks were named for.

Even though it's shiny, the skin of silkies is as tough as any other shark's.

SILKY SHARK STATS

AVERAGE LENGTH
7 to 8 feet (2.1 to 2.4 m)

MAXIMUM LENGTH
10 feet (3 m)

RANGE
warm waters of the Atlantic,
Pacific, and Indian oceans

LIFE SPAN
more than 20 years

DIET
tuna, small fish, squid, and crabs

NICKNAME
net-eater, because it often tears up seine nets
set out to catch tuna

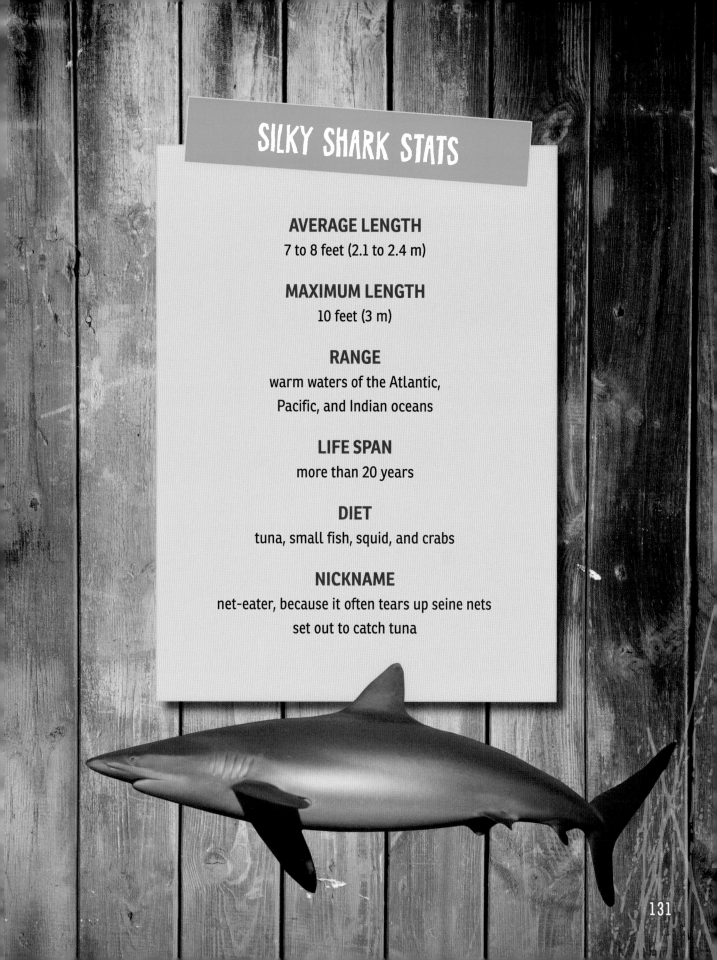

Suddenly, the water around the boat began to boil with jumping fish frantic to escape the sharks. Four jacks landed in the boat. Then there was a huge POW! Sharks were ramming the hard underside of the raft.

The boat had drifted directly over the bait ball, and the small fish were trying desperately to hide beneath it. For 20 minutes sharks slammed into the bottom of the boat, trying to catch the fish cowering there. Only the wooden planks on the floor of the boat separated the sharks from the crew.

More small fish tried to escape by leaping out of the water. Then the divers saw an amazing sight—a silky shark bolted right out of the water, its mouth crammed with fish.

Finally the sun disappeared below the horizon. Ten minutes later, the water around them was quiet. Only gentle waves rocked the boat. The sharks were gone—but not forgotten. It was the closest that Jeff and Asher had ever come to being shark bait.

PROTECTING THE CREATURES OF SHARK ISLAND

Many sharks swim great distances across the world's oceans yet return regularly to a home base, a place such as Costa Rica's Cocos Island. The waters around Cocos Island provide a sanctuary where sharks are supposed to be safe. It is illegal for sharks to be caught by fishermen within the national park. Where sharks are protected, they usually live long enough to have young so that there will be more sharks in the future.

Jeff has visited Cocos Island many times in the past 15 years. Over that time he has seen the number and size of the sharks shrink, devastated by illegal fishing. Some species have been fished out altogether.

a young blacktip shark hooked on a longline

Jeff has made friends with fishermen who work near the protected waters around Cocos Island. He's lived aboard their boats for weeks at a time, filming the fishing practice of longlining in order to make the public aware of what's happening. Fishermen roll out miles of fishing line late in the afternoon and haul them back into the boat at sunrise. With as many as 2,000 baited hooks, longlines are meant to catch legal fish such as tuna. But they often snare unintended creatures as well, such as seabirds, sea turtles, and sharks.

Asher attempts to remove a fishhook from a caught sea turtle. Sea turtles are protected from being hunted in Cocos Island National Park.

Jeff uses his skills as a photographer to try to save sharks.

Some longline fishermen, like those around Cocos Island, specifically target sharks. These fishermen might stay out for three weeks at a time. Their small boats have little room to store their catch and no ice to keep it fresh. So they cut off the fins to sell and toss what's left of the maimed sharks overboard.

Unable to swim without their fins, the injured sharks sink and die a slow death.

Fishing for sharks is illegal within the boundaries of Cocos Island National Park. But Jeff says that it is only in the last 10 years that environmental laws meant to protect sharks there have been enforced.

SHARK FIN SOUP

In most seas of the world, sharks are captured specifically for their fins. The fins may be sold for as much as $600 a pound for shark fin soup, a delicacy in some Asian cultures. At a cost of $65 to $150 a bowl, the soup usually is served only on special occasions.

An estimated 26 million to 73 million sharks are killed every year to meet the demand for shark fin soup. It's hard to imagine 73 million of anything. Think of it this way: The 2012 U.S. census found that the entire population of people under the age of 18 in the United States numbered about 73 million. It's a big number.

Jeff has spent many hours in places around the world filming the gruesome results of shark finning in order to help stop the practice. Jeff's photographs have told the story in publications in more than 25 countries. Environmental organizations working on conservation campaigns use the photos to educate people about what is happening to sharks. This effort is helping to make a difference, as people realize the harm that eating shark fin soup is doing to the ocean's top predators. More places, including the United States, China, and Hong Kong, are passing laws to stop the sale of shark fin soup. Shark finning is being banned in many countries.

If these laws are enforced, there may still be a future for sharks.

Shark watchers spend hundreds of millions of dollars a year on dive trips to swim with sharks, but those who make money from ecotourism usually are not the same people who fish for sharks.

If people can help local fishermen earn more money by keeping sharks alive for tourism than they can make killing them for soup, there may still be a future for sharks.

One of the main reasons Jeff travels the world photographing sharks is to show how awesome they are. Sharks don't have the "cute" appeal dolphins or seals have, but they need protecting just as much. Without sharks, sick animals would spread disease, injured fish would suffer longer, and decaying carcasses would litter the ocean and wash up on shore.

If everyone stops viewing sharks as sea monsters and instead learns more about the important role they serve in our oceans, there may still be a future for sharks.

As painful as it is to see a shark without its fins, Jeff hopes his photographs will motivate people to help stop the cruel practice of finning.

THE FUTURE FOR SHARKS

About 400 to 450 different kinds of sharks have been discovered so far, and Jeff Rotman has photographed around 100 of them. When Jeff looks back over his career as an underwater photographer, he says, "The ocean is a different place from the one in which I started diving 40 years ago. It will never be the same again, but with the help of people who care about the ocean, who want to see sharks and other sea creatures thrive, perhaps it will be wonderful still."

Jeff Rotman is where he loves to be—
surrounded by sharks.

AUTHOR

Mary M. Cerullo has been teaching and writing about the ocean and natural history for 40 years. She has written more than 20 children's books on ocean life. Mary is also associate director of the conservation organization Friends of Casco Bay/Casco Baykeeper in Maine, where she lives with her family.

Mary with granddaughter Taylor

PHOTOGRAPHER

Jeff with sons Matthew and Thomas

Jeffrey L. Rotman is one of the world's leading underwater photographers. Diving and shooting for more than 40 years—and in nearly every ocean and sea in the world—this Boston native combines an artist's eye with a naturalist's knowledge of his subjects. His photography has been featured on television and in print worldwide. Jeff and his family live in New Jersey.

GLOSSARY

barbel—a whiskerlike feeler on the jaws of some fish

breach—to leap partly or completely out of the water

cartilage—a strong, rubbery tissue that connects bones in people and animals; in sharks, the entire skeleton is composed of cartilage

cephalic fin—head fin

copepod—a shrimplike zooplankton that is a key animal in ocean food webs

dorsal fin—back fin

dugong—a relative of a manatee, which lives along the coastlines of the Indian and Pacific oceans

ecotourism—visiting a place that has unspoiled natural resources, while being careful to have minimal impact on the environment

extinct—no longer living

filter feeder—a marine animal that strains plankton out of the water

finning—the practice of cutting off a shark's fins and discarding the shark, often still alive, back into the ocean

marine sanctuary—a section of the ocean where a government has placed limits on human activities to protect the habitat and marine life

nocturnal—active at night and resting during the day

parasite—an organism that lives on or in another organism in order to get nourishment or protection

pecking order—an animal behavior where one animal demonstrates it has a higher status among its kind by actions such as eating first or taking the best resting place

pectoral fin—side fin

plankton—single-celled plants and animals that drift with currents

reef—a formation on the ocean floor composed of the skeletons of coral animals

skate—a member of the ray family that doesn't have a venomous spine at the base of its tail

spiracles—small holes through which some animals breathe

wahoo—a prized game fish known for its tasty flesh and speed

INDEX